Fluent Chinese: the complete p

by Judit]

Copyright © 2015 Judith Meyer

All rights reserved.

ISBN: 1511848847

ISBN-13: 978-1511848848

DEDICATION

For my parents, who supported me in this and many language-learning endeavours

CONTENTS

	Acknowledgments	i
1	Getting Ready	1
2	Starting From Zero	9
3	Tourist Level	21
4	Upper Beginner	27
5	Intermediate	35
6	Advanced	41
7	Fluent	47
	About the Author	51

ACKNOWLEDGMENTS

This book would not have been possible without the help of Katerina Barone-Adesi, Chuck Smith, Marina González, Sophia Chen, Professor Man Gao of Dalarna University and the many wonderful Chinese people who encouraged me on my long journey.

1 GETTING READY

China's long history and ancient culture, its many contributions to science, its current economic strength and huge population all make it a very interesting part of the world on which to focus. But even if Chinese was spoken by only one million people in a remote part of Canada, I'd still want to learn the language. I have studied more than a dozen languages and Chinese is the most fascinating one I know.

The characters called to me, promising the revelation of secrets that few Westerners know. As a child, I'd trace them without comprehension. As a beginner, I'd doodle them in the margins of all my notebooks at school. As a fluent Chinese speaker now, I count myself lucky to be able to write in such a beautiful script.

Though to be honest, it's not quite as beautiful when I write it. I never had a talent for drawing and art. It's not necessary to be good at drawing, or good at remembering pictures, in order to learn Chinese. Nor is it necessary to be good at singing in order to master the Chinese "tones". Even tone-deaf Chinese people can express themselves perfectly. More about this in the next chapter.

For now, let's focus on what you need to get ready to learn Chinese.

1. Materials

You do not need to buy brushes, ink and calligraphy paper – though if you want to, be my guest. Modern Chinese people use pens and write in regular lined notebooks or on computers.

Get a blank lined notebook that you'll only use for your notes on Chinese. I personally like to use artsy notebooks (Paperblanks or custom-made) with covers that remind me of the language I'm studying. For me, writing something into a beautiful notebook like that is a reward in itself, so it makes me want to study.

Also make sure that your computer can handle Chinese characters - google "Chinese support Windows 8", "Chinese support OSX" or similar, as there are too many possibilities for me to describe them all here. On Youtube, you can find neat video tutorials on how to set up your system for Chinese.

Don't buy a Chinese course just yet. I found that free online courses are often superior to the courses you'll see in stores (especially Rosetta Stone, which is over-hyped to unsuspecting beginning language learners) and I will list a lot of my favorite resources. Give them a try; they're free after all. If you don't like them, you can still try one of the paid options.

2. Motivation

No matter what certain marketing geniuses will tell you, learning Chinese will never be fast and it's certainly not something you can do between lunch and hockey today. If you're going to learn Chinese, you have to be ready to stick with it in the long run. Expect it to be months until you can get by in everyday situations, years until you're an expert.

There will definitely be times when you're ready to thrown in the towel. So save up some strength right now: make a list of all the reasons you want to learn Chinese and all the awesome things you'll be able to do once you speak fluent Chinese. Ideally, you'll write this list on a decorative piece of paper and hang it somewhere visible. If you don't have that luxury, at least write this list at the beginning of your Chinese notebook. (Did I mention you should start a fresh notebook dedicated to Chinese?) Consult this list whenever you feel overwhelmed with Chinese and - like an "*expecto patronum*" spell - it will dispel some of the fear and allow you to start moving towards your target again.

3. Time

Your success in learning Chinese depends entirely on whether you'll be able to regularly make time for Chinese.

Pedagogic and neurological studies have shown that you cannot study something in one week and expect to remember it in the next. Our brain works in stages and to move something from the short-term to the long-term memory, and keep it there, you have to do regular reviews. Once you know a word, you can gradually increase the time between reviews – from 1 day to 3 days to 7 days to 2 weeks to one month or similar. The exact distances depend on a lot of factors (computer software like Anki will schedule it for you) – but this still means that you should at least glance at new words every day, not just every week. The longer you wait to do this necessary review, the more you will have forgotten, which means that you'll have to re-learn the words, which means that you have less time to spend on pushing your Mandarin forward. People who attend one two-hour class a week and don't do anything else will generally spend at least 80% of the time on re-learning what they could have remembered from the previous sessions, if they had done proper review. So their learning speed is only 20% of what it could be. It will take them 5 years to learn as much as others might learn in 1 year.

Review doesn't have to take much time. Depending on the number of new words you're learning, even 5 minutes / day might be enough. If you have a flashcard app on your smartphone (recommended) or use paper flashcards, you can easily fit these in while doing other things, for example while waiting for the water to boil, while microwaving something, while waiting for a phone call, or while using public transport. The key then is to have your flashcards immediately available, carrying them on your person (a good reason to have them on your smart-phone), so that you can use these short moments.

If you use this approach, you don't have to schedule your review time. Just be sure that if you haven't managed to fit in a review during the day, you'll do it quickly before going to sleep. There is emerging evidence that studying something just before sleeping is particularly good for memorization, assuming you're still awake enough to focus.

As for the longer study sessions and language practice, you do need a schedule, especially at the beginning, when you're not used to making time for your language study. And I even recommend keeping a diary or at least a spreadsheet record of when you studied and for how long, because our brain often deceives us and remembers the last study session to have been more recent than it was. Besides, tracking your hours will also allow you to track how close you are to your goal.

When giving things some thought, we do actually have a lot of potential time for language study, even next to a full-time job. Here's one of my day schedules with all potential language-learning times written in:

6.00 – ca. 7.00 Get up, have breakfast, get ready

7.00 – 7.30 Study the textbook if I have time

7.30 – 8.00 Go to work, doing flashcards on my iPhone while on the bus or listening to a podcast

8.00 – 12.30 Work

12.30 – 1.30 Have lunch. Often I'd have some foreign language conversations with my co-workers over lunch, because I worked at an international company.

1.30 – 5.00 Work

5.00 – 5.30 Go home, occasionally studying more vocabulary or podcasts, usually just relaxing and clearing my head

5.30 – 7.30 Spend time with family, surf the internet, reply to e-mails etc., have dinner

7.30 – 8.00 Do dishes and other cleaning while doing self-talk exercises or listening to podcasts

8.00 – ca. 10.00 Spend time with family & friends and/or watch a movie, ideally in a foreign language with subtitles

10.00 – 11.00 Do some light reading, ideally related to my target language or a book in one of my advanced languages

11.00 – 6.00 Sleep

I obviously don't use all of those time slots every day. I usually just use one or two of them. Even if you can only find time for one 2-hour study session every week, maybe on the weekend, that is enough to make some progress, as long as you also do a 5-minute review on most days. (If you cannot commit to even two hours a week, I recommend delaying your Chinese project until you have more time, or going with a European language, which won't require as much time.)

To be sure you actually have this time that you now envision, best mark it in your calendar.

To recap the TODOs:

- get blank lined notebook to be used exclusively for Chinese

- install Chinese Support on your computer

- make a list of your reasons to learn Chinese

- decide how to handle flashcards / reviews

- identify one or more weekly time slots for your Chinese study and mark this time in your calendar

Judith Meyer

2 STARTING FROM ZERO

Congratulations! Coming to Chinese as a beginner is an exciting time in any language lover's life. That being said, your goal is to leave the beginner stage as soon as possible. Why?

1.   As a beginner, you can't do many fun things with the language yet, so it's easy to give up. Once you can understand TV shows, read websites and have long conversations with people, you won't give up on the language anymore.

2.   It's easy to forget a language completely if you pause while you're at the beginner stage, but if you pause while you're at the intermediate or advanced stage, you won't forget as easily. Real Life has a way of interfering sooner or later, forcing you to pause your studies, so aim to be beyond the beginner stage by then. Work intensively at the beginning, using any opportunity to do another few minutes of your

target language, and then relax once you've hit the intermediate stage.

Now, this is how you start learning Chinese:

First focus: pronunciation

Chinese characters don't give away much about their pronunciation, so almost all textbooks will provide Chinese pronunciation using the Pinyin system. That makes Pinyin the very first thing that you should learn and also the most important thing you can learn as an absolute beginner.

Pinyin is a way to note Chinese pronunciation using the Latin alphabet. For example, to say "Hello" is

你好！ Nǐ hǎo!

"Nǐ hǎo" is the Pinyin spelling of the Chinese sounds. In a phrasebook for English tourists who can't be expected to learn the Pinyin system, you might find the same phrase spelled „knee how" instead, because the pronunciation of the Pinyin letter I corresponds to the English EE in "knee" and the Pinyin AO is similar (though not quite the same) as the English OW sound. Learn to pronounce every letter and every letter combination in Pinyin. This will be your most important goal at this stage, because the system is entirely regular and it will enable you to learn new Chinese words from any source, even when there is no recording available.

Mastering Pinyin will also sharpen your ear towards important distinctions that you might otherwise not notice in the audio, for example the fact that Chinese distinguishes between consonants pronounced with your tongue touching your teeth and consonants pronounced with your tongue pointing upwards and back (linguists say 'retroflex').

In Pinyin, CH and Q are pronounced identically (similar to English CH in "chat"), except that for CH your tongue is pointing upwards and back, touching the roof of your mouth, and for Q it is touching your teeth.

In Pinyin, ZH and J are pronounced identically (similar to English J in "journalist"), except that for ZH your tongue is pointing upwards and back, touching the roof of your mouth, and for J it is touching your teeth.

Similarly, you want to point your tongue upwards and back in order to pronounce a flawless Chinese SH, but for X the tongue touches your teeth.

This is an explanation of Chinese sounds that you won't always find in textbooks, so bookmark it.

Tones

When I tell people that I speak Chinese, a lot of them seem to think that the tones are really difficult. They are very surprised when I tell them that the tones are quite simple, we even have them in English!

This story will help you remember the tones and even remember their numbering. (Chinese people refer to the tones as "1st tone", "2nd tone",

"3rd tone", "4th tone"):

Imagine a very young German boy who sees an airplane in the sky. He points at it and says "da da" as young children do (you can imagine him saying "there there" instead, but "da" is an actual Chinese syllable, so it works better). In saying so, he is using the 1st Chinese tone, the even tone. However, the boy's mother does not see what he's pointing at, so she asks "da?" ("there?"). The tone that we use for questioning is called the 2nd tone in Chinese. Our voice rises a little, so that we can tell the difference between someone saying "This is for me." and "This is for me?" So the 2nd tone in Chinese is also called the 'rising' tone. Back to the boy and his mother. The boy is not impressed with his mother's inability to see, so he mocks her question: "da?!" This tone, the falling-rising tone, is the 3rd tone in Chinese. Finally, the boy strongly affirms "da!" ("there!"). For such a strong affirmation, or also for commands to dogs, we English speakers naturally use the 4th Chinese tone, the falling tone. So in this story you can find all 4 Chinese tones, in the right order, and in a context where you'd use them in English.

The key difference between tones in Chinese and in English is that Chinese uses tones much more often. Every Chinese syllable has a tone assigned to it and pronouncing it with a different tone can change the meaning. Learning the tones really means learning to use them consciously, so that you don't use a rising tone in Chinese questions anymore but instead you are able to apply a rising tone to whichever syllable you want. Don't worry too much though, the chance that you'll accidentally offend someone by using the wrong tone for a word is quite slim – Chinese people are used to foreigners getting the tones wrong. It impedes comprehension, especially once you use more than just beginner sentences, but it's not something they'll fault you for.

Back to Pinyin: you may have noticed that "Nǐ hǎo" has accent marks on the i and a. In Pinyin, the accent marks directly correspond to the tone. If you look at the accent mark here (they're both the same) and try to perceive it as a sound wave going from left to right, it seems to start high, go down and then go up again. This is exactly what happens with the tone. It's the third tone. Here's how to spell the 4 tones of "da" as in the story: dā dá dǎ dà. In all cases, the accent mark shows you exactly how the tone will change: stay the same, rise, fall-rise or only fall. This is very convenient and one of my favourite features of Pinyin. It's not convenient to type though, especially on cellphones, so you may see people write da1 da2 da3 da4 instead, putting the tone number after each syllable.

Resources for Pinyin

As a beginner starting from scratch, your most important goal should be to master the Pinyin inside and out. This will lay the foundation for everything else. These are the free sites I recommend for learning Pinyin and learning to pronounce Chinese:

https://chinese.yabla.com/chinese-pinyin-chart.php – there are so few possible syllables in Chinese that you can actually list them all. This is the list, and the best part is that you can click on any of them in order to listen to the sound, pronounced with every tone.

http://www.pinyinpractice.com – once you have familiarized yourself with the sounds of Chinese, use the various exercises on this site in order to challenge yourself to identify which letter or which tone you're hearing.

http://learning.chinese.cn/wordbook – computers are marvelous things! This site can give you automatic feedback on your Chinese pronunciation, especially the tones. Record yourself and strive to get a 90% or 100% match on each syllable.

Learning essential Chinese : course recommendations

In order to reach the next stage, the level where you can function as a tourist, you don't need much. The Chinese government estimates that you only need about 150 words. You also need next to no grammar, because Chinese is very simple – they don't have changing verb forms like *I am, you are, he is* or *I write, he writes, he wrote, he has written*, they don't have filler words like a/an/the, they don't even have a plural! (1 glass, 2 glass, 3 glass...) Almost every other major language has much more grammar than Chinese. So really your problem boils down to learning the vocabulary (not too easy, since the words look like nothing you've ever seen before) and accepting some weird ways of phrasing things, which sound suspiciously like the broken English used in Asian martial arts movies. Just keep in mind that for Chinese, that's the natural way to say things and English in turn sounds strange to them.

To learn the basic vocabulary and a lot of useful sentences in which you can use it, I recommend www.LearnYu.com, my own project, which automatically determines which words you know well enough, which ones you still need to study and which sentences will help you the most at your current stage. There are many language courses for this level though, so if you prefer, download the free Foreign Service Institute materials (audio drill based), use Teach Yourself or Colloquial, use Michel Thomas... the most important criterion is that you should enjoy using the course, or at least not dread your study time. Also, don't hesitate to switch materials if one of the courses gets boring (or gets too difficult).

I usually use self-study materials rather than group classes, because they give me the freedom to study whenever I have time and to progress as fast or as slowly as I need. However, self-study materials don't replace the need to work with a teacher or native speaker occasionally. You can get really cheap tutoring (starting at $4 for 60 minutes!) via Skype from the teachers at http://www.italki.com/?ref=794526 . Have a tutoring session at least every 7-14 days, depending on how quickly you advance in the course.

The tutors don't replace the self-study, they enhance it: ask them questions about things you didn't understand, practice the kind of dialogs you learned and occasionally ask them to provide extra exercises or to find an easy song for you to learn or the like.

Tutors also keep you honest: if you know that there is a session coming up, you are less likely to skip language study. If you find yourself at a really low stage in motivation or very busy with other things, schedule several tutor classes ahead of time in order to ensure that you keep studying the language and it isn't relegated to the back burner and forgotten.

Using books with the traditional Dialog – Vocabulary – Grammar – Exercises split

A lot of language courses have this split: first one or more dialogs, each with a set of vocabulary to learn, then one or more sections of grammar explanations, then exercises, maybe a cultural section at the end. No matter if you're using Teach Yourself Chinese, Colloquial Chinese, Langenscheidt Chinese or Assimil Chinese with Ease, you will recognize this split. For most courses I recommend finishing each lesson within 3 days of starting it, so that you don't have much insecure and incomplete knowledge floating around your head. With the Assimil books, I recommend trying to finish each lesson on the same day you started it, because the lessons are much shorter.

Here are the steps I'd take for every lesson:

1. Read through the lesson completely. Don't focus on what you don't understand, just get a general idea of everything

2. Look at the grammar in-depth and compare the explanations to how the grammar is used in the dialogues. Do the exercises that relate to that grammar point right then (don't do all the exercises at the end). If something is difficult, also look for additional exercises on the same topic for example in another textbook, in a grammar book or online.

3. Memorize the vocabulary. I often use Anki (free software from www.ankisrs.net) to study vocabulary; it's really effective. Some people prefer Memrise (www.memrise.com) or traditional paper flashcards. If there are exercises relating to the vocabulary, do them now.

4. Study the dialogs until you can understand them without referring to the vocabulary list or grammar.

5. Listen to the dialog audio several times, perhaps even many times. Vary what you do while listening: sometimes follow along in the book, sometimes try to understand without seeing the words in front of you, sometimes speak along with the dialog in order to improve your pronunciation. If you wind up knowing much of the dialog by heart (not something to aim for, but a good side effect), that's great, because you'll be ready to re-use those lines in your own conversations.

Supplementary materials

This is the core study routine, the one you can do when you are wide awake and have some time to spare. There are other things you can do when you're less able to focus or have less time. For example, I also like to use songs at this point. They make language study more interesting. Listen to songs in Chinese, for example on an internet radio station or on Youtube. If you like the song, look for the lyrics and try to figure out what they mean (you can google song title + "english translation" or use Google Translate). Then listen to the song several times while reading along or while looking at the translation. This helps you pick up more vocabulary. You can also use www.singchinesesongs.com - a site especially for learning Chinese through songs. They have song recommendations, Pinyin, translations and even Pinyin karaoke for you to sing along.

Other than songs and textbooks, you can also use language-learning podcasts at this stage, for example ChinesePod.com, CSLPod.com or the like. These are generally not good enough as stand-alone language courses, but they are good as review / to pick up more vocabulary.

At the beginner stage, you cannot say much, but you should still use whatever you know as much as possible. If going to a Chinese restaurant, say "Hello! How are you?" in Chinese even if that's the only Chinese you know. Then, when you know more, add other phrases, like "Number 20 please. - Thank you". Even later, start chatting to the waiter about where he's from, how long he has lived here, what dishes he can recommend, and so on.

The important thing is to **start using Chinese**, even if it's just a few canned phrases. When the brain notices you using the language, it realizes that the language is important to know and it will remember things better.

A note on learning characters

I do not recommend learning characters at this point. Focus entirely on becoming an expert user of Pinyin and on getting used to the Chinese sentence structure. Even the HSK (official exam) for levels 1 and 2 does not require you to recognize any characters. If you cannot contain your curiosity though, you may want to read some texts on how Chinese characters evolved – without consciously trying to memorize any at this point. Once you are ready to memorize characters, consult the equivalent section in the next chapter.

Potential reward

To reward yourself for completing this stage of your Chinese journey, take your family or friends to a Chinese restaurant and impress them by ordering in Chinese for everyone.

Judith Meyer

3 TOURIST LEVEL

You have taken the first step towards mastery of Chinese and you can already say a few things in Chinese, enough to get by as a tourist in China. How to improve from here?

Your next step is to become someone who can talk about simple daily things in Chinese. For example, this is the level you should have if you're planning to stay with a host family in China, in order to be able to communicate with them about what's going on. This is also the point where you can start to have conversations in Chinese with friends.

Words and grammar: measure words

To get there, you need to learn approximately as many words as you already know, if the people designing the official HSK test are to be believed. So another 150. That's not too scary. You can probably even stay with the course you're already using and just keep doing lessons. If need be, get a second textbook / second volume of the textbook you've been using.

The role of grammar will be slightly larger, but nothing you can't handle. Tenses will come up. "Measure words" will come up. Those might be the most annoying part of Chinese grammar, something even advanced learners can still get wrong. Essentially, measure words are like the words "bottle" or "glass" in English. In English, you cannot say "1 wine", you have to say "1 bottle of wine" or "1 glass of wine". Same for bread: it's "1 loaf of bread", never "1 bread". Chinese has the same concept, but they apply it much more rigorously: every single thing has to be measured in some way before you can count it. For example, the Chinese would say "1 flat-thing of map, 2 flat-things of maps, 3 flat-things of maps" - never "1 map, 2 maps, 3 maps". The tricky part is to figure out which measure word will be used for the thing you want to count (there are categories, like "flat thing" or "electronic thing" or "small round thing" and the like). As a beginner, you can get away with using the common counting word 个 " ge" for basically everything. Measure words will never be a source of misunderstanding, so it's not worth it to invest too much energy in this if you still make a lot of bigger mistakes.

Pronunciation: Sandhi

As you should be completely comfortable with Pinyin syllables, this is a good time to ensure that you can also do two-syllable combinations well (Wordbook can help you with that, too), and to read up on the Sandhi – the times when syllables change their actual (not written!) pronunciation because of the melody they're in.

The most important Sandhi rule is the one about two 3rd-tone words following each other, as in "wǒ jiějie" (my older sister): if there is no pause between the words, then the first word should be pronounced with the 2nd tone, even though it remains written as the 3rd tone. This improves the flow, that's why the rule only applies when not pausing. Also read up on the Sandhi rules about the word bù (not) and the word yī (one).

Learning characters: how to

I recommend starting to learn characters now, though technically it's possible to delay until the next level. The thing is, there are some words and grammar topics that you'll learn in this level and the next one that make a lot more sense when you know the associated characters – for example the difference between the three particles 的, 得 and 地. They are all pronounced "de" but they have very different grammatical functions, so it helps to be able to see which one you're dealing with.

To learn the characters, Chinese people write them over and over again. This transfers the characters into muscle memory – the memory that you're using when typing your PIN at the ATM. Your fingers know how to trace your PIN number even if it would take you a second longer to recall the number into your brain.

Muscle memory works well for Chinese people because they handwrite the characters so often, so the muscle memory is regularly reinforced. Muscle memory needs a lot of reinforcement. This is a problem for Chinese people nowadays because the younger generation mostly uses computers and cellphones to write Chinese, so they are forgetting how to write the characters. As Westerners, we stand even worse chances of remembering the characters through muscle memory alone. It is therefore best to also involve the brain.

First, stop seeing the characters as a series of almost-random strokes. Familiarize yourself with the basic elements and their inate meaning, if you haven't done so already. This will also help you distinguish 王 (king) 壬 (ancient burden) and 玉 (jade) or 土 (ground) and 士 (knight). You will notice that the vast majority of Chinese characters are not new, they consist of two or more of the basic elements. If you know the basic elements, you can then construct a mnemonic to link the elements to their meaning, a little story to help you remember or even a downright explanation. For example, the character 林 meaning "forest" consists of two trees, and the character 明 meaning "bright" consists of sun and moon - not difficult to remember, is it? The character 休 meaning "to rest" consists of a person and a tree - mentally fix the idea of an exhausted hiker resting against a tree and you'll never forget this character again. This works for complex characters as well, and for each character you can choose into how many parts you split it, e. g. if you want to think of 偷 meaning "thief" as (person + making a canoe) or as (person + Chinese roof + moon + knife) - I went for the latter, with a story involving a thief on the roof of a house in moonlight, knife in hand, in order to climb into one of the windows and steal stuff.

Stories can be colorful, absurd, racy, nonsensical even, as long as you personally find them memorable.

For the purpose of learning a large amount of characters this way (I memorized almost 2500 in one non-intensive year), it makes sense to go from basic characters to more complex ones, also so that you don't have to memorize all possible basic elements at once. Unfortunately, quite a lot of frequent words involve characters that are complex combinations of 4 or more elements, so it is non-obvious which order you should learn characters. It is possible to go this path alone; www.zhongwen.com will give you an analysis of each character's components and you can make stories from that. But I don't recommend it, because then you'll encounter the issue of having one peg word corresponding to several characters, or inadvertently learning out-of-use characters, or learning complex characters before learning the parts that they're made of.

I recommend getting a book to guide you. If you're learning simplified characters (the most common set, used in mainland China and Singapore), get Alison and Laurence Matthews' "Learning Chinese Characters". They propose pictures and stories to go along with every character and the stories will even help you remember the pronunciation and the tone if you choose. This book covers about 1000 characters, roughly sorted in order of appearance in textbooks (!); it's really great as a textbook companion for a beginner with little prior knowledge of characters and methods.

If you're learning traditional characters (the ones used in Taiwan and many expat Chinese), or if you don't like Matthews' book for some reason, get William McNaughton's "Reading and Writing Chinese". This is available in both simplified characters or traditional characters. It is more seriously, with less pictures or stories, but also proposes a very good order for learning the characters and also gives you good peg words to use in your stories. This book covers more than 2200 characters even, almost enough to take the highest-level Chinese exam, the HSK 5.

When I was blasting through Chinese characters, I additionally made character flashcards in Anki, to ensure that I wouldn't forget what I learned. I found it particularly motivating to use the HanziStats plugin, which showed me what percentage of the various HSK levels I had covered and what percentage of frequency lists I had covered. It was great as a progress bar and occasionally it also prompted me to learn more, if I saw that I only needed 4 more characters in order to cover 100% of the HSK level 2 vocabulary.

Potential reward

You won't finish the characters at this level (1000 characters is well into "Advanced" territory by Chinese government estimates and 2000 characters is "Fluent"), but you can already enjoy recognizing characters on signs and restaurant menus.

Have a "let's mangle Chinese" dinner! Invite your Chinese-speaking friends, both native and non-native speakers, for a light Chinese conversation over dinner. If you invite fellow learners, you can be sure that the vocabulary level of the conversation won't be too difficult. It's also easier than having a conversation with someone, because with 4-6 people at the table, you don't have to do so much to keep up the conversation, you have more time to think of what you want to say.

4 UPPER BEGINNER

You are now an upper beginner student reaching for intermediate. As an intermediate, you will be able to talk about most things concerning you, including your studies and your professional life, albeit on a basic level using simple words.

There are textbooks specifically for the intermediate stage. I admit I don't generally use them, because I'm not a fan of textbook study. Instead, I get a cheap community tutor from www.italki.com and I focus on one topic per session.

For example, for one session I might try to talk about traveling. At the beginning of the session, it's difficult because I'm missing so much vocabulary, but I ask the tutor to teach me every word I need and then we keep talking about traveling for the rest of the session, trying to keep using the same words and trying to exhaust the topic more than we might in a normal conversation. At the end, phrases like "I have never been to X" or "I want to go to Y" or "I really enjoyed my time in Z" should be second nature, you should be able to use them spontaneously and fluently without thinking.

This is the idea of topic-based fluency: choose a topic, spend 60 minutes with a tutor becoming absolutely fluent in anything you might want to say about it, then choose another topic, rinse and repeat. Eventually you will be able to talk fluently about every topic that interests you.

If you ever want to master a particular topic "out of order", before textbooks would normally cover it, you can use the same approach. Maybe pre-learn some key vocabulary, then have one or two tutoring sessions talking only about this topic, picking up a lot of relevant expressions on the way, and feel relatively confident talking about the topic by the end. I successfully used this approach in order to learn to talk about the crisis in Greek before I even knew how to order a hotel room, and I used it to become confident talking about language learning in Indonesian within just 6 weeks, going on stage to give a talk about how to learn languages at the end of the challenge.

Supplementary materials for this stage

In addition to working with a coursebook and/or tutor, keep going through "Learning Chinese Characters" as your basic staple, but also increasingly seek out fun, authentic materials such as Chinese songs, short video clips and movies (with English subtitles).

I can particularly recommend the following resources to supplement your learning at this stage:

www.singchinesesongs.com – learn Chinese songs and sing along

www.gurulu.com – read & listen to news in very simple Chinese (choose texts for HSK 2 or possibly 3)

www.fluentu.com – watch interesting short videos with subtitles in Pinyin and English, then learn vocabulary from them

http://english.cntv.cn/program/learnchinese/happychinese/ - watch the series "Happy Chinese", a sitcom especially made for Chinese learners

http://thetravelingprogrammer.com/files/ChineseCharacterChallenge/ - review your knowledge of Chinese characters

The Zhongwen Popup Dictionary or Perapera Popup Dictionary as a plugin for your browser (find it in Browser Extensions) – it will allow you to read Chinese websites quite comfortably, whenever you hover over or click on a word it will give you the translation.

Learning grammar: two resources

Chinese grammar can get a bit tricky at this stage, because you are learning things that don't have a direct equivalent in English. However, rest assured that soon you'll be in easier territory again.

If your textbook's grammar explanation is hard to follow, check out the Chinese grammar wiki (http://resources.allsetlearning.com/chinese/grammar/), which has good, detailed explanations about most topics.

For extra exercises, check out http://www.ctcfl.ox.ac.uk/Grammar%20exercises.htm .

Learning vocabulary: similar-sounding words

At this point, a lot of people run into the problem that words all start to sound the same and that it takes longer to memorize words. For this, it's important to look at the characters that make up words and to understand each character. This is akin to looking at the English word "happiness" and understanding that it derives from "happy" and "ness", "ness" being a common way to form abstract nouns. Or looking at "democracy" and, through some research, understanding that it originally came from the Greek words "demos" (= common people) and "kratos" (= rule, strength). Understanding the origin of Chinese words is the key to learning them quickly and not confusing them.

Additionally, if you find that you're always confusing two particular sounds (e. g. q and ch), or mis-remembering the tones, you should consider adding a mnemonic for these. The book "Learning Chinese Characters" suggests using a giant for tone 1 (high and stable), fairy for tone 2 (rising), teddy for tone 3 (falling-rising) and dwarf for tone 4 (falling). So then, if you want to remember that 楼 lóu, the Chinese word meaning "building", uses the 2nd tone, you'd imagine a building with a fairy flying around it. If you don't like these archetypes, you could also use colors, or famous people – as long as you're consistent and you create memorable pictures, the words will be easy to remember.

I do not generally create such mental pictures for all words I study, only for the ones that don't stick in my head on the second or third time I review them.

Learning vocabulary: remembering words in conversation

Another common problem at this stage is conversation speed, in both directions. When your teacher is only using words you know, you may nevertheless not understand him/her until you have quietly repeated the words to yourself, but then you understand everything. This is a speed problem rather than a memorization problem.

To help you overcome this, make recordings of your teacher (or use pre-recorded audio from various textbooks or online sites) and play them on your computer. If you're using Windows Media Player or almost any audio player, there is a menu option to slow down the sound. Slow it down to 70% or however slow you need it to be in order to understand the words, then gradually speed it back up again until you're able to understand this at full speed. As a bonus, use the same menu option in order to play the sound file at a faster-than-normal speed. Once you are able to understand the recording at 130% speed, the regular recording will sound like slow motion. Do this enough times and even your teacher will appear to be speaking comfortably slow.

Similarly, you are probably experiencing the problem that it takes you too long to form sentences, so you pause a lot in conversation or stutter. This is happening because you are not yet used to speaking a lot of Chinese. Neuroscientists have found that the human brain is unable to retrieve words from the internal dictionary at the speed we need them in conversation. So why are we still able to speak our native language without too many pauses? Because of something called 'chunking'.

A chunk of words is more than just one word but less than a full sentence. Usually chunks are 2-4 words long. Chunking means that when you say "I am hungry, let's go have fried noodles", your brain does not look for the words for "I", "am", "hungry" and the like, it probably has a stored memory of chunks of words: "I am hungry", "let's go", "have", "fried noodles". Your brain finds these chunks of words in its internal dictionary and therefore only needs 4 'dictionary lookups'. But language learners' brains don't know how to chunk yet, so they actually look up every word by itself. That means twice as many look-ups, and each look-up also takes longer than for a native, so on the whole you need much more time to crank out the same phrase.

There is no way around it, you have to allow your brain the time to see & store chunks. You need to hear or say "wǒ è" a lot of times before your brain stores it as a chunk. You can speed up the process though. Here are some ways:

- Put chunks of 2-4 words on your flashcards, rather than one word per card. Make sure that these 2-4 words are usually heard together; don't combine random words.

- Challenge yourself to write X sentences using the same chunk.

- Have tons of conversations or self-talk exercises, so that the most common phrases become chunks that you can recall without effort.

- Select a few chunks beforehand and try to use each of them several times in your next conversation.

If you binge-watch a Chinese TV series, pay attention and you may also pick up some of the most common phrase chunks. Time-wise it's smarter to work on your vocabulary directly of course, but TV series, movies and online videos are a good way to add some extra Chinese to your day when you're too tired to study.

Potential rewards

When you're ready to graduate to Intermediate stage (and pass the HSK level 3), you can reward yourself in several ways:

- Plan a vacation in China.

- Organize a Chinese karaoke night. If you live in a big city, you can probably find an actual Asian-run karaoke bar with separate rooms for groups of friends. If not, use Youtube. Just search Youtube for the name of a Chinese song and the word "karaoke" or "hungry" and you'll have your own private karaoke machine.

- Read the short novel "三人行 – Annas Sommer in Beijing" by Yi Zhou and Marion Rath. Even though half the title is in German, the text of this book is completely in Chinese (simplified characters, no Pinyin). It's the easiest book I'm aware of that feels like a book you'd actually want to read, not a series a textbook texts. It uses approximately 600 characters. Being able to say "I read a complete book in Chinese" is a great way to prove to yourself how far you've come already!

Judith Meyer

5 INTERMEDIATE

As an intermediate, you have a unique chance to start delving into Chinese culture, including art, songs, movies and TV shows, which are often unavailable to English speakers.

If you aren't binging on a Chinese TV series yet, start doing so now. I particularly enjoyed these ones:

三国演义 – A war epic relating the Three Kingdoms period of Chinese history, starting in 169-280 AD. As a history epic it doesn't contain much useful vocabulary, but it helps you understand a lot of cultural references, because the series is based on one of the four greatest treasures of Chinese literature.

步步惊心 - Modern time-travel romance with an insight into life at the Qing dynasty imperial court.

温州一家人 – Tracing a rural family's path through the economic reforms and turmoil of the 1980s.

There's also "Travel in Chinese", a series produced by CCTV with the goal of being both a travel magazine and a way to improve your Chinese. The other series I listed are made for native speakers. Find "Travel in Chinese" at
http://english.cntv.cn/program/learnchinese/travelinchinese/index.shtml

While you can enjoy a lot of Chinese TV already and have interesting conversations with Chinese friends, reading is likely to remain a problem for a little while longer.

There are two issues with reading at this stage, even assuming you have a text that doesn't involve many unknown characters:

Issue #1: Perceiving Chinese text as an image

Chinese is a character-based writing system and it doesn't use spaces. Both of these mean that when you see a text in Chinese, it looks like a picture, or like a concrete wall. This is different from other languages: if I gave you a text in Catalan, you could see the words that it consists of, you could quickly skim it to find the word "democràcia" and you could understand a few words like this. Not so with a Chinese text: a Chinese text remains opaque at first glance. If you start reading it, you may find that you understand almost all the words, but this isn't obvious when you're confronted with a wall of Chinese. How do you train your eyes to perceive Chinese texts as similarly transparent as Catalan ones?

Do skim-reading exercises. Print out a text of which you know the approximate content and then drag your eyes along it vertically, looking for a particular word that you know should be in there. Do not read the text! That's why you're supposed to look over it vertically, to not even be tempted to read. Your goal is to be able to find relevant words in a wall of Chinese text. This will be an incredibly useful ability for future Chinese reading, especially when you're trying to navigate the Chinese web and want to get a quick overview of pages, rather than having to read everything from start to finish.

You can even do this exercise with texts that are beyond your current level, such as newspaper texts. Open an article on the English version of www.project-syndicate.org, read it, and then use the language dropdown at the top in order to get the same article in Chinese. (Available for most articles except the very latest ones.) Then skim for words that should appear based on your knowledge of the English text.

If you're binging on a Chinese TV series, you can use this technique in order to follow the discussion of the series in Chinese forums: find a relevant question on the question & answer site www.zhihu.com (or simply search on the Chinese Google www.baidu.com), then skim the text until you see the characters that interest you, then use a hover dictionary or the software Wenlin in order to read what it is written.

Issue #2: Reading way too slowly

Reading speed is also a very common problem among Chinese learners of this stage and an urgent one to fix, especially if you're studying at a university where they expect you to read tons of texts in

Chinese. If you can read a page of English text in 1-2 minutes, you may need 5-10 minutes per page of Chinese text, or even more if you haven't yet read anything except textbook texts.

Your Chinese reading speed is slower than the speed at which people would say the same text aloud (in English, the opposite is true). Take advantage of this and use texts for which you have matching recordings, for example texts from textbooks that you're not using, lessons on texts on Gurulu.com, easy readers that come with an audio CD (e. g. by the Italian publisher Hoepli), even Chinese audiobooks if you're not afraid of the unknown vocabulary. If you listen to the recording as you read the text, your eyes will automatically be moving over the Chinese text faster. Read the same text without listening to the recording later and try to keep up the same speed.

A more extreme approach is to paste all Chinese text you work with into Google Translate and use the loudspeaker button in order to listen to a computer voice pronounce the text as you read along.

Apart from using audio to pace your Chinese reading, you can also use the general speed-reading exercise on Tim Ferris' website; it works for foreign languages just as well as for English and it only takes 20 minutes: http://fourhourworkweek.com/2009/07/30/speed-reading-and-accelerated-learning/

Finally, to improve your reading ability in Chinese you can also use the free lessons offered by the Defense Language Institute, at https://gloss.dliflc.edu .

Potential Rewards

Here are some things you can look forward to doing after graduating from this level:

• Watch the hundreds of excellent Chinese TV series for which there are no English subtitles available (Chinese subtitles will help you understand)

• Read Sinolingua's Abridged Chinese Classic Series, which are classic works of Chinese literature that have been simplified for learners, even including Pinyin and audio recordings.

• Read Western books that have been translated into Chinese (they tend to be easier) or interesting non-fiction books like for example "搭车去柏林" (hitchhiking from Beijing to Berlin) or "闯入美国主流" (about language-learning and going to America)

• Sign up for Dalarna University's debate class "Chinese in Speech and Conversation", which is a lot of fun and free for EU/EEA citizens. www.universityadmissions.se

Judith Meyer

6 ADVANCED

At the advanced stage, you can communicate freely with native speakers on a wide range of topics. You may have to use simpler words, but you can always get your point across.

Using native-like expressions

Your main problem, apart from the need to learn more vocabulary, is that you're not using the language as a native would. You are still relying too much on the English way of phrasing things (e. g. saying 不会按时来 rather than 来不及) and are missing idiomatic ways of saying things. This is a problem that all language learners have when reaching the advanced stage, also in European languages, though in European language it's less obvious because a lot of expressions are the same across European languages.

There are some books promising to teach you Chinese idiomatic expressions, especially the dreaded Chengyu, but if you're learning expressions from a book, you are more likely to use them in an inappropriate context than not. In my opinion there is no way to learn them except through reading and hearing a lot of Chinese. Getting exposure to a LOT of real authentic Chinese (not the textbook variety) should be your main goal at this stage.

In terms of learning expressions that you will be able to adopt as your own, conversations are best, TV series and movies are second best and books should be used with caution, as the expressions may be too bookish.

For conversations, I wouldn't pay a tutor anymore because it's not work to have a conversation with me at this stage. A tutor only makes sense if he helps you study, not for simple conversations. Instead, join a local expat meet-up, language meet-up or language exchange in order to find people with whom you can speak the language. Meetup.com knows of such events in most cities, but google is also your friend, and often these groups also have Facebook pages.

When watching TV series and movies, be sure to watch them with Chinese subtitles at this stage. This is very easy for Chinese compared to other languages: a lot of movies and even online short films already have embedded Chinese subtitles. When not referring to English, you'll learn so much more!

Regarding books and other written materials, there is quite a big difference between spoken Chinese and written Chinese, if your source isn't a bunch of teenagers on WhatsApp. Reading may not help your ability to sound like a native in conversations, but it is definitely the way to go if you want to improve your own written expression in Chinese. One site that you can use to improve your understanding of written Chinese is www.foreigncy.org . They provide vocabulary and guide you to understand Chinese news articles. Also keep using https://gloss.dliflc.edu for this, looking at the higher-level items.

Understanding fast spoken Chinese

The radio is a good source at this stage, too. Last.fm and other sites allow you to receive a lot of Chinese radio stations, as well as foreign radio stations broadcasting in Chinese, for example the BBC, Voice of America, Deutsche Welle and Radio Canada all have broadcasts in Chinese. When you first start on these, you may find them a bit daunting. (Less so if you've been using the higher-level lessons at www.cslpod.com, which are taught in Chinese.) You may want to experiment with different stations and different programs in order to find one with moderators that speak relatively comprehensibly and slowly.

Alternatively, you can use a trick, which will help your brain to quickly get used to hearing fast Chinese: make recordings of a Chinese radio broadcast (or download from the site if possible) and play them on your computer. If you're using Windows Media Player or almost any audio player, there is a menu option to slow down the sound. Slow it down to 70% or however slow you need it to be in order to understand the words, then gradually speed it back up again until you're able to understand this at full speed. As a bonus, use the same menu option in order to play the sound file at a faster-than-normal speed. Once you are able to understand the recording at 130% speed, the regular recording will sound like slow motion.

Feeling stuck

As you progress further and further, you may have the uncomfortable feeling of being stuck, of not getting any further.

This is because your rate of progress becomes less and less visible as you go on. To give you an example: if you have a vocabulary of 100 words and you study another 100 words in one intensive week, that is an improvement of 100%. You will immediately notice that you can say twice as much as before. However, if you have a vocabulary of 2000 words and you study another 100 words, that is only an improvement of 5% and it won't be as noticeable – even though in both cases you put in the same amount of hard work. This is the curse of the higher levels.

In order to make your progress more visible (because you are progressing, you're just too good already to notice it), there are several possibilities and you should use them all:

- Log the amount of hours you put in. They say that Chinese requires ca. 2200 hours to master to a professional level (I think it can be done in less). Well, start counting. Any hour you spend, even if it's watching a movie with Chinese subtitles, will bring you closer to the goal, so it is motivating to see your hour count go up. Treat it like a progress bar on the computer.

- Occasionally note the amount of words you know (Anki can tell you). You may not immediately notice the impact of learning another 100 words when you already know so many, but the impact is there and if you keep learning more words, you will eventually be in a situation that drives home how much you learned while you thought you were on a plateau.

- Learn words / expressions around one specific topic and then, a short while later, go back to that topic (talk about it with friends, write about it on www.lang-8.com, whatever). You will notice all the new words you have at your disposal. If unconvinced, you can even do a before-after picture: record yourself trying to talk about the topic before, then study, then record yourself again once those words have sunk in. You should be able to speak more fluently and express yourself better.

That being said, if objective criteria show that you're actually not progressing, for example if you don't manage to increase your vocabulary count or you don't manage to learn a new grammar point, review the tips on learning vocabulary and grammar that I mentioned in the earlier chapters.

Jealousy

A lot of people find the intermediate and advanced stage in Chinese frustrating because they had a better experience with European languages. When learning a European language such as French or Spanish, everything gets easier at the advanced stage, because that's when you're tapping into a common European set of words like *president, democracy, publish*, and so on, which are very similar in most

European languages. In fact, as an intermediate student you may find it easier to read a Spanish newspaper than to read a Spanish children's book! Even Indonesian and Swahili borrowed a number of these words.

Chinese does not have this advantage. The writing system makes it very difficult to borrow foreign words, so you'll have to learn Chinese words for all these concepts (at least you can relate to the individual meaning of the characters making up such words). Don't get frustrated if you have to spend longer at the advanced stage in Chinese than for other languages. There is also the matter of culture. At the advanced stage, you are increasingly confronted with cultural references – and unlike for European languages, chances are very low that you'll understand those references. See it as a chance to discover. Learning about Chinese culture is one of the reasons you're in this, right? The way is the goal.

Rewards

The sky is your limit. Whatever your goal was in learning Chinese, you can probably do it, now that you've graduated from 'advanced' level. Original literature may still be a challenge, but practise with an on-hover dictionary, a parallel text or an easier text first and you will soon be reading even that. Reward yourself by doing whatever you always wanted to do in Chinese.

7 FLUENT

Enjoy life! :-)

Seriously, you have reached a level in Chinese that few Westerners will ever reach and you should lean back and enjoy it.

There is of course no point at which you're "Done" with a language, especially not one as different from ours as Chinese is. There will always be things you don't know, cultural references you don't get, expressions you hear for the first time. But being fluent means that these occasions are rare enough that you can take them in stride and just learn whatever you need when you need it. No avenue is completely closed to you; you know enough words to get started on anything and learn the rest of the words as you go.

Maybe you want to delve into Chinese regional varieties now or explore 文言文.

Maybe you want to study Chinese Linguistics or Modern Chinese Literature. Dalarna University has online beginner classes for both, taught in Chinese, and they're free for EU citizens: www.universityadmissions.se . These courses involve doing Powerpoint presentations in Chinese and even writing a short scientific essay in Chinese at the end. If that sounds daunting (it did to me), don't worry, it is doable at this stage. It will help your Chinese grow.

You could also listen to the 50+ Chinese university courses that are offered on www.coursera.org , ranging from philosophy to computer science classes. I think they are more difficult language-wise than the Dalarna courses, because Dalarna courses are intended for non-native speakers.

If you are aiming for the HSK 6 exam, get a test preparation book and work through the exercises.

Other than that, buy Chinese books that look interesting. Watch Chinese TV series and movies that sound interesting. Talk to interesting people. By using your Chinese for things that you actually care about, you will gradually – maybe unnoticeably – keep building your Chinese.

In learning many languages, if there's one thing I found it's that languages adapt to the use we have for them. Both in the good sense and in the bad sense: if you speak a language fluently but then only use it to order food at a restaurant, you will eventually lose most of what you knew except the food vocabulary. On the other hand, if you speak a language less-than-fluently and regularly have to give Powerpoint presentations in that language, your language level will improve so that your presentations are really good after a while (but you may still have trouble with food vocabulary). It is nice to say that you know enough Chinese read literature, but this ability will fade within a few years if you don't actually read literature in Chinese. So use the language, realize your dreams in it, make it part of your life and it won't ever leave you.

Good luck and best wishes,

         Judith Meyer   April 2015

Judith Meyer

ABOUT THE AUTHOR

Judith Meyer is a Berlin-based polyglot and computational linguist. She speaks more than 12 languages and has participated in the creation of language courses for GermanPod101, GreekPod101, DutchPod101 and ArabicPod101. She also published a number of ebooks and books and is now working on www.LearnYu.com, a Chinese course based on artificial intelligence.

Judith loves to help others succeed in their language-learning and to encourage anyone to give it a try.

Learn more about Judith and her current projects and get free language-learning advice at www.learnlangs.com .

Printed in Great Britain
by Amazon